VICTIMIZATION
Victory Over
the Victim Mentality

JUNE HUNT

ROSE PUBLISHING/ASPIRE PRESS

Torrance, California

ROSE PUBLISHING/ASPIRE PRESS

Victimization: Victory over the Victim Mentality
Copyright © 2015 Hope For The Heart
All rights reserved.
Aspire Press, a division of Rose Publishing, Inc.
4733 Torrance Blvd., #259
Torrance, California 90503 USA
www.aspirepress.com

Register your book at www.aspirepress.com/register
Get inspiration via email, sign up at www.aspirepress.com

Printed in the United States of America
010115RRD

CONTENTS

ear Friend,

Powerless. Fearful. Broken. Hopeless.
Do these words describe you and the way you've always felt deep down inside? If your truthful answer is yes, then this study is for you. Each of these words portray how a victim feels, and rightfully so. But did you know that those feelings can continue long after the abuse has stopped? They can creep into every relationship, encouraging you to forfeit your true feelings for the sake of being a "people pleaser." They can shackle you like chains on a prisoner, making you feel trapped—like a victim—when in fact, you are free. You are a former victim. You have overcome ... or at least you can.

I'm going to be very candid with you right from the start. I've been a victim of abuse and I've been a victim of the victim mentality. It took a long time for me to accept the fact that I was still living like a victim, but once I did, I was able to find true freedom that no victimizer can steal—*a freedom that lasts forever.*

How clearly I remember the day I realized that I, a grown adult, was still living like a helpless child. It was a number of years ago when a friend of mine called unexpectedly. *"June,"* she said. *"I've been reading a new book, and I would like for you to listen to this list of characteristics. Think about yourself as I read."* She went down the list and, one by one, the characteristics matched me. The author was painting an almost perfect portrait of me—my relationships, my working style, even my innermost feelings!

Then my friend revealed the purpose of the list. *"I didn't want to tell you this at the beginning, but the list has to do with adult children of alcoholics."* Though I'm not from an alcoholic home, I did fit many of the characteristics. In truth, I was amazed by how many described me *to a T*. Having had a counseling ministry for years, I knew why. Children with alcoholic parents feel powerless, especially if the drinking leads to abuse.

Even though I did not grow up with an alcoholic parent, I did grow up with someone who made me feel powerless. I felt incredibly helpless around my father, who ran our family like a dictator—and not even a benevolent one! He was an abusive man who caused my family to rally together just to survive against him. Harsh and brutal, my father devastated my sense of self-worth. Even his "minor offenses" burned deep in my heart.

I recall one time when my sister Helen and I were playing chess on the living room floor. Then my father entered. *"Quit playing chess!"* he roared. *"It's not as scientific as checkers!"* I knew it wasn't a major thing, but to see him towering over us, making ridiculous demands, made me boil inside. My first thought was: *What do you mean checkers is more scientific than chess? Who cares?* I was extremely angry, but I couldn't say anything. I knew that whatever he said was "right." I felt powerless.

By the time I was a teenager, my father's verbal and emotional abuse had warped my entire worldview. All my girlfriends were boy crazy, but I wasn't. I remember the day we learned that Ricky Nelson was coming to Dallas to perform at the Cotton Bowl. The announcement aired on the radio when we were all piled in the car. *"Let's go! Let's go!"* they cried. I had to work just to put a smile on my face.

Although we didn't end up going, I'll never forget how I felt driving down the road that afternoon. I couldn't understand: *Don't you realize how heavy things are in the world? How serious things are? How can you even think about going to a concert?* I didn't understand how they could be so happy over something that I thought was so silly. Happiness was not a frame of reference for me. But I never told a soul. For years, I didn't tell anyone about the things that went on in my home.

I found other ways to cope, including avoiding my father. If he came through a door, I hid in the closet. If there wasn't a closet, I hid behind the door. I became a peace-at-all-costs person, even lying to keep my father from getting upset. I worked hard at the things I knew would please him, hoping, just once, to hear, *"I love you."* But I never heard those words ... not from him.

I grew up being fearful—and that fear penetrated my adult life. I was even afraid of friendships. Although I had precious friends who were nothing like my father, I still felt and thought like a victim. I lied about things without reason. I kept my loved ones at arm's length. My victim mentality continued to plague me, even when it came to my relationship with God—my heavenly Father, who had shown His love for me so many, many times before.

Something changed in me that day on the phone with my friend. I realized that I had been trapped, no longer by my father, but by my own refusal to stop living like a victim. I decided then to let God set within me a new perspective, to allow Him to change my victim mentality and ultimately to change my heart and my life.

My prayer for you is that through the pages of this study, you too will allow God to make that kind of liberating change in you. Today is God's day of freedom for you. He has a path for you—a good and perfect plan for your life—that no amount of abuse or mistreatment can destroy. I pray that as you look at the truth of His Word, you will find in Him the power to stop living as a victim and to start living as the person God made you to be: His precious child—forgiven, redeemed, and set free.

Yours in the Lord's hope,

June

June Hunt

"Blessed is he whose help is the God of Jacob, whose hope is in the LORD his God ... who remains faithful forever. ... The LORD sets prisoners free, the LORD gives sight to the blind. The LORD lifts up those who are bowed down."
(Psalm 146:5–8)

VICTIMIZATION
Victory Over the Victim Mentality

Here they come again—those painful memories that permeate your heart and pummel your thoughts and emotions. You feel caught like a frightened bird in a cage with no way to freedom. Yet it happened so long ago.

Do you live your life coping with a crippling crisis from your past, hoping to somehow get beyond it, to forget it? Well, the good news is that God wants so much more for you than just to cope. He wants to help you overcome your painful past and conquer the destructive patterns that have developed in your life as a result of your past victimization. He wants you to grow in maturity through His grace and to reach out and help others in similar pain.

Feeling powerless doesn't have to be permanent. God wants to set you free from the cage that has far too long held you captive and robbed you of peace! He offers you His power for healing and for changing. And when you experience true healing and personal transformation, you also receive true freedom. Like a bird out of a cage, you can experience freedom today and have bright hope for tomorrow! All because of the fact that ...

"It is for freedom that Christ has set us free. Stand firm, then, and do not let yourselves be burdened again by a yoke of slavery." (Galatians 5:1)

DEFINITIONS

She is the daughter of a king, but she becomes a desolate woman. Her position guarantees a lifetime of honor and recognition, but instead she spends most of her life in seclusion and disgrace.

Tamar's earlier years are characterized by beauty and innocence, which both captivate and torture a certain young man, her half brother, Amnon. *"Amnon became so obsessed with his sister Tamar that he made himself ill. She was a virgin, and it seemed impossible for him to do anything to her"* (2 Samuel 13:2).

But Amnon's shrewd cousin comes up with a plan that makes the impossible possible.

"For your ways are in full view of the Lord,
and he examines all your paths.
The evil deeds of the wicked ensnare them;
the cords of their sins hold them fast.
For lack of discipline they will die,
led astray by their own great folly."
(Proverbs 5:21–23)

Jonadab counsels Amnon, *"Go to bed and pretend to be ill. When your father comes to see you, say to him, 'I would like my sister Tamar to come and give me something to eat. Let her prepare the food in my sight so I may watch her and then eat it from her hand'"* (2 Samuel 13:5). Amnon has no trouble figuring out the rest of the plan.

King David attends to his "sickly" son Amnon and dutifully honors his request to beckon Tamar to his bedside. Tamar prepares cakes and brings them to Amnon, but instead of grabbing hold of the cakes, he grabs hold of Tamar. *"'No, my brother!' she said to him. 'Don't force me! Such a thing should not be done in Israel! Don't do this wicked thing. What about me? Where could I get rid of my disgrace? And what about you? You would be like one of the wicked fools in Israel. Please speak to the king; he will not keep me from being married to you'"* (2 Samuel 13:12–13).

Tamar's voice of reason goes unheeded, and Amnon, determined to satisfy his fleshly appetite, proceeds to forcibly rape his half sister. *"He refused to listen to her, and since he was stronger than she, he raped her"* (2 Samuel 13:14). In so doing, Amnon proved himself to be *"one of the wicked fools in Israel!"*

"In his arrogance the wicked man hunts
down the weak, who are caught in the
schemes he devises."
(Psalm 10:2)

▶ A victim is a person who experiences adversity, who is powerless to change the situation.[1]

Examples: A victim of neglect as a result of alcoholic parents, an unwanted divorce, infidelity, spiritual abuse, suicide, elder abuse, stalking, or sexual harassment.

- Tamar was clearly the victim of Amnon. And as his victim, she experienced all three of the following definitions of a victim:

▶ A victim is a person who is tricked or duped.

Example: A victim of robbery, identity theft, fraud, kidnapping, cult entrapment, and other dishonest schemes

▶ A victim is a person who is injured, destroyed, or sacrificed.

Example: A victim of incest, domestic violence, rape, satanic ritual abuse, drunk driver, homicide, natural disaster

▶ A victim is a person who is subjected to oppression, hardship, or mistreatment.

Example: A victim of any verbal, emotional, sexual, physical, racial, or economic abuse

> "People cry out under a
> load of oppression;
> they plead for relief from
> the arm of the powerful."
> (Job 35:9)

Tamar's tragic loss of innocence would be but the first in a string of abuses committed by Amnon, who after maliciously victimizing Tamar, *"hated her with intense hatred. In fact, he hated her more than he had loved her"* (2 Samuel 13:15). He commands her to get out and has a servant put her out when she refuses to leave. He repudiates the notion of taking her as his bride, which the Law required, and tells the servant to bolt the door behind her.

▶ A Hebrew word in the Old Testament that refers to a victim is *chelekah*, which means "hapless, unfortunate, the unlucky."[2]

"He [the wicked man] *lies in wait near the villages; from ambush he murders the innocent. His eyes watch in secret for his victims ... "* (Psalm 10:8).

▶ Old Testament translations of the word *victim* are ...

- The slain
- The dead
- The killed
- The wounded
- The victim
- The defiled
- The casualties
- The slaughtered

According to these translations, Jesus was a willing victim of our sins, the innocent laying down His life for the guilty. *"He was pierced for our transgressions, he was crushed for our iniquities; the punishment that brought us peace was on him, and by his wounds we are healed"* (Isaiah 53:5).

Tamar was devastated by Amnon's heartless disregard for her feelings and wishes, her plans and her dreams. And the deep disdain he felt toward her after forcing himself on her was more than she could bear.

To express her deep sorrow and shame, Tamar tore her richly ornamented robe, which symbolized her status as a virgin daughter of the king, and placed ashes on her head. And ...

> "She put her hands on her head and went away, weeping aloud as she went."
> (2 Samuel 13:19)

▶ The victim mentality is a mind-set in which a person who was once a victim continues in old thought patterns that foster feelings of powerlessness, even when the victimization has ended.

▶ The victim mentality causes individuals to see others as powerful but themselves as weak and powerless.

▶ The victim mentality leads those who were genuinely powerless to stop abuse in the past to assume the same powerless state in the present. In order to fully embrace the future that the Lord has planned for them, this faulty assumption needs to be replaced with God's truth.

▶ The victim mentality can consciously or subconsciously be used to deny responsibility for a person's present actions. The individual continues in self-destructive attitudes and actions while blaming others for the undesirable results. Victory requires a new mind-set.

"We demolish arguments and every pretension that sets itself up against the knowledge of God, and we take captive every thought to make it obedient to Christ." (2 Corinthians 10:5)

QUESTION: "What will help me overcome a victim mentality?"

ANSWER: You can overcome a victim mentality by changing the way you see God and the way you see yourself in relationship to Him. This will then result in changing the way you see yourself in relationship to others and to events in your life. As a past victim, you may have been defenseless, but now you are no longer without power.

"In all these things we are more than conquerors through him who loved us." (Romans 8:37)

God is a God of love, and He created us for love relationships. Therefore, He hates violence and He takes up the cause of victims who fall prey to violent words and violent deeds. He will execute justice one day on behalf of all victims. And woe to those who will face the judgment of God—He who sees all and knows all from whom nothing is hidden.

"Nothing in all creation is hidden from God's sight. Everything is uncovered and laid bare before the eyes of him
to whom we must give account."
(Hebrews 4:13)

Be assured ...

▶ God hears the cry of the battered and abused (Psalm 10:17).

▶ God holds the victim of abuse in the palm of His hand (Isaiah 41:10).

▶ God will rescue the victim of abuse and violence (Psalm 72:14).

▶ God confirms the victim's value and worth (Luke 12:6–7).

▶ God brings good out of the evil deeds of others (Proverbs 16:4).

CHARACTERISTICS OF THE VICTIM MENTALITY

At the heart of the victim's wounded emotions is the feeling of powerlessness, feeling unable to make healthy choices in circumstances and relationships. Left with a damaged sense of self-worth, unhealed victims of abuse develop unhealthy beliefs and behaviors. And because of a past lack of control, some victims have a hidden fear of being controlled in the present. Therefore, they themselves may become overcontrolling.

Other victims resign themselves to not being in control and have a hidden fear of not being controlled. Therefore, they may become codependent. Both of these positions with their unresolved emotional difficulties can produce spiritual and physical side effects.

The cry of a victim's heart is often ...

"Have mercy on me, LORD, for I am faint; heal me, LORD, for my bones are in agony."
(Psalm 6:2)

WHAT IS the Profile of a Victimized Person?

Victimizers leave their innocent victims with abiding feelings of rejection and personal defectiveness. The constant fear that their "stains" will be exposed causes victims to develop destructive ways of relating to others. A victimized person typically exhibits several of these characteristics:

A —**AMBIVALENT** — Experiences conflicted emotions about pain and pleasure and gives mixed emotional signals to others

B —**BETRAYED** — Expects rejection and is unable to trust or have faith in God or others

U —**UNEXCITABLE** — Lacks passion for both good and bad, merely seeks to be free of conflict with others, flat affect without emotional highs or lows

S —**SELF-ABSORBED** — Consumed with self-protection and unable to be sensitive to others

E —**EMOTIONALLY CONTROLLED** — Disengages from true feelings and becomes blind to the feelings of others

D —**DEPENDENT ON SELF** — Seeks to be in control because of a reluctance to depend on God or others

The constant cry of many victims is: *"My soul is in deep anguish"* (Psalm 6:3).

Victim Mentality Checklist

Some of the most frequent and fervent statements made by victims of abuse are listed below. Place a check mark (✓) beside the ones that apply to you.

☐ I am a worthless and unlovable person.

☐ I am bad if I feel angry.

☐ I am better off with bad love than no love at all.

☐ I am defective.

☐ I am responsible for the behavior and feelings of those around me.

☐ I am terrible because I hate my victimizer.

☐ I am wrong for having needs.

☐ I must be dependent on others because they are wiser and stronger than I am.

☐ I must be unlovable if people I care for reject me.

☐ I must keep peace at any price.

☐ I need the approval of other people in order to be happy.

☐ I will be loved if I am good.

☐ I will never let anyone get close enough to me to hurt me again.

☐ I will never measure up.

☐ My feelings are less important than the feelings of others.

☐ My mistakes only confirm my worthlessness.

Those who have been extensively victimized generally struggle with severe emotional side effects such as ...

#1 LOW SELF-WORTH[4]

- Accepting abuse
- Accepting blame
- Accepting condemnation
- Accepting injustice
- Being critical of self and others
- Being desperate for approval
- Being unable to set boundaries
- Being unable to accept compliments
- Being a people pleaser
- Being defensive

If you struggle with feeling devalued and insignificant, remember Jesus' words.

> "Consider the ravens:
> They do not sow or reap, they have no
> storeroom or barn; yet God feeds them.
> And how much more valuable you are
> than birds!" (Luke 12:24)

#2 DEPENDENCY[5]

- On food
- On drugs and/or alcohol

- On people
- On religion
- On physical appearance
- On social status
- On financial security
- On personal abilities
- On material possessions
- On professional success

Addictions are mood-altering whether through a chemical (alcohol), a behavior (gambling), or a person (codependency). If you have been victimized, you need to let the Lord be your Need-Meeter, your Deliverer.

When you humble your heart before Christ and invite Him into your life, He will be your power source to deliver you from any addiction.

> "For he will deliver the needy who cry out, the afflicted who have no one to help." (Psalm 72:12)

#3 FEARFULNESS[6]

- Of abandonment
- Of rejection
- Of failure
- Of affection
- Of intimacy
- Of authority figures
- Of God

- Of unexpected changes
- Of unfamiliar places
- Of unpredictable situations

Fear triggers the release of adrenaline in the body that propels us to action—action often called "fight, flight, or freeze." It is a natural emotion designed by God. However, prolonged fear or fearfulness is not designed by God, for fearfulness means living in a state of fear or having a spirit of fear.

"God has not given us a spirit of fear, but of power and of love and of a sound mind."
(2 Timothy 1:7 NKJV)

#4 EXCESSIVENESS

- In control
- In seriousness
- In work
- In organization
- In relationships
- In appearance
- In safety
- In rules
- In details
- In thoughts

The danger is that the excessive attention or action often becomes so strong that the person feels powerless to control it. But the One who created the mind can certainly reprogram it through the power of His Spirit and the power of His Word.

Therefore, God instructs us to ...

> " ... offer your bodies as a living sacrifice, holy and pleasing to God —this is your true and proper worship. Do not conform to the pattern of this world, but be transformed by the renewing of your mind. Then you will be able to test and approve what God's will is— his good, pleasing and perfect will."
> (Romans 12:1–2)

#5 Compulsiveness

- About perfectionism
- About responsibility
- About daily routines
- About cleanliness
- About orderliness
- About personal rituals
- About repeated victimization
- About dieting
- About exercise
- About locking doors

Those who feel controlled by compulsive behaviors need to know that ...

> "God will meet all your needs according to the riches of his glory in Christ Jesus."
> (Philippians 4:19)

Physical abuse impacts the whole person—body, soul, and spirit. Those who are subjected to repeated victimization often suffer from some of the following physical and mental problems.

▶ **Disorders**

- Substance abuse or addictions
- Anorexia, bulimia, or overeating
- Self-injury or self-endangerment
- Dissociation or splitting

▶ **Memory disturbances**

- Memory blocks
- Flashbacks
- Memory loss
- Body memories

▶ **Sexual difficulties**

- Loss of libido, impotence
- Promiscuity, prostitution
- Sexual identity confusion
- Defensive reactions to touch

▶ **Sleeping disruptions**

- Nightmares
- Insomnia, restlessness

- Fear going to bed or to sleep
- Awaken frequently to avoid sleeping too soundly

The pressing prayer of many who have experienced victimization is ...

> "Listen to my cry, for I am in desperate need; rescue me from those who pursue me, for they are too strong for me.
> Set me free from my prison, that I may praise your name." (Psalm 142:6–7)

WHAT ARE Some Spiritual Side Effects of Victimization?

While victims suffer emotional, physical, and mental side effects of being abused, those who are repeatedly victimized also struggle with obstacles to their spiritual growth. They ...

▶ **Possess a knowledge of God but little personal experience of God**

- Know God is all-powerful, all-knowing, and ever-present.
- Know God is a force to be reckoned with
- Know God is eternal and sovereign

▶ **Are angry with God for not stopping the abuse**

- Think God is responsible for the bad things that have happened to them
- Think God is cruel and unloving

- Think God is unfair and unjust

▶ **Have difficulty forming an intimate relationship with God**

- Struggle with being honest and open with God

- Struggle with believing the promises of God

- Struggle with giving their hearts and lives to God

▶ **Distrust God for allowing the abuse**

- Consider God to be unrestricted and undiscerning in the use of His power

- Consider God to be a liar

- Consider God to be undependable

▶ **Fear God's anger and displeasure**

- See God as impossible to please

- See God as punitive and vindictive

- See God as condemning

▶ **Have feelings of rejection and unworthiness**

- Feel God has abandoned them

- Feel God has ascribed no value to them

- Feel God has thrown them on the garbage heap

▶ **Project the attributes of their abuser onto God**

- Believe God is hurtful and insensitive

- Believe God is selfish and controlling

- Believe God is inconsistent and unpredictable

▶ Seek to gain God's approval

- Hope God will bless them for their sacrificial giving

- Hope God will bless them for their church-related activities

- Hope God will bless them for their service to others

▶ Harbor warped, negative perceptions of God

- Perceive God as being distant and disinterested

- Perceive God as being indifferent to their pain

- Perceive God as being unavailable

Some spiritual strugglers become so embittered ...

> "They say to God, 'Leave us alone!
> We have no desire to know your ways.'"
> (Job 21:14)

Others, however, choose to reach out in faith to lay hold of the promises of God.

"The gospel ... is the power of God that brings salvation to everyone who believes" (Romans 1:16).

"Come! Let the one who is thirsty come; and let the one who wishes take the free gift of the water of life" (Revelation 22:17).

"Come to me, all you who are weary and burdened, and I will give you rest. Take my yoke upon you and learn from me, for I am gentle and humble in heart, and you will find rest for your souls" (Matthew 11:28–29).

All of us have developed ways of avoiding unpleasant situations and responsibilities, but those operating out of a victim mentality have become experts at self-protection.

Developed early in life through modeling or sheer creativity, these skills are learned responses and ways of relating that were necessary for surviving abusive situations.

Often operating subconsciously, these behaviors can undermine non-abusive relationships and sabotage the healing process.

Only by walking in the truth of God's Word through the power of His Spirit within us can we overcome.

"Teach me your way, LORD, that I may rely
on your faithfulness; give me an undivided
heart, that I may fear your name."
(Psalm 86:11)

Survival Personalities

▶ **The Dependent** gives up personal responsibility in many areas of life and uses helplessness to get support from others. This disguise, adopted for protection, sends the message "I need you," but in adulthood it becomes a powerful means of controlling and manipulating others.

▶ **The Pleaser** has the motto "peace at any price." By constant compliance with the wishes or desires of others, this individual pays a high price for approval and acceptance. As an adult, the pleaser has lost a great deal of personal identity.

▶ **The Fixer** has low self-worth and attempts to fix it by becoming responsible for and fixing others. Fixers are often seen as very loving, self-sacrificing, and spiritual—though often these traits are merely for show, used to avoid addressing their own needs.

▶ **The Performer** appears highly competent and seems to have it all together. A perfect performance for every act is the performer's unattainable goal. Although there is a certain amount of personal satisfaction in doing so much so well, this person is inwardly paralyzed by the fear of being found to have inadequacies.

▶ **The Controller** feels secure only when in control. As an adult, the controller comes across as self-assured, always right, and, for the most part, looking good. A fear of vulnerability is what makes this wounded lamb act like a lion.

▶ **The Martyr** is a great and constant sufferer. Anyone who has been abused needs and deserves the compassion of others. The martyr, however, controls others by continuing to elicit compassion for having experienced devastating abuse.

Rather than using self-designed, self-defeating survival skills, the Bible presents another perspective ...

> "Since we are surrounded by such a great cloud of witnesses, let us throw off everything that hinders and the sin that so easily entangles. And let us run with perseverance the race marked out for us, fixing our eyes on Jesus, the pioneer and perfecter of faith. For the joy set before him he endured the cross, scorning its shame, and sat down at the right hand of the throne of God." (Hebrews 12:1–2)

WHAT ARE the Victim's Broken Boundaries?[8]

Because of past physical and emotional abuse, victims may continue to have difficulty establishing and maintaining personal boundaries. And adults who relate to others out of a victim mentality often have difficulty being appropriately honest and assertive. They validate the words spoken by Isaiah the prophet ...

> "Justice is driven back, and righteousness stands at a distance; truth has stumbled in the streets, honesty cannot enter."
> (Isaiah 59:14)

If you think you have difficulty establishing and maintaining appropriate boundaries, take the following test.

Checklist for Broken Boundaries[9]

☐ Do you find it difficult to make decisions and stick with them when opposed?

☐ Do you feel you must seek opinions from others before making a decision?

☐ Do you feel hesitant to give your opinion when asked?

☐ Do you fear expressing what you really feel?

☐ Do you lack confidence in your own convictions?

☐ Do you avoid certain people because you fear embarrassment?

☐ Do you find it difficult to maintain eye contact with another person?

☐ Do you find it difficult to ask others for help?

☐ Do you do favors for others even when you know you shouldn't?

☐ Do you avoid asking people to return overdue items they have borrowed?

☐ Do you need a great deal of assurance from others?

☐ Do you have difficulty pointing out situations that are unfair?

☐ Do you ever say *yes* when you want to say *no*?

If you checked any of these boxes, you may be operating with a victim mentality. Be aware: *"Fear of man will prove to be a snare, but whoever trusts in the Lord is kept safe"* (Proverbs 29:25).

Someone who is "codependent" is dependent on another person to the point of being controlled or manipulated by that person. We should have a healthy "interdependence" on others in the sense that we should value and enjoy each other, love and learn from each other, but we should not be totally dependent on each other.

An interdependent relationship involves a healthy, mutual give-and-take where neither person looks to the other to meet each and every need. However, many people who have experienced victimization form misplaced dependencies on others. These kinds of relationships are not healthy. God intends for us to live in total dependence on Him, realizing He will work through others to meet some of our needs but not expecting or looking to others to do so.

Over and over, the Bible portrays how godly people learn to have a strong dependence on the Lord rather than a weak dependence on each other. The apostle Paul said we should ...

" ... not rely on ourselves but on God."
(2 Corinthians 1:9)

▶ Codependent people may appear capable and self-sufficient, yet in reality they are insecure, self-doubting, and in need of approval.

- This need for approval can result in an excessive sense of responsibility and a dependence on people-pleasing performances.[10]

However, the Bible says our primary focus should not be on pleasing people, but rather on pleasing God. *"We instructed you how to live in order to please God, as in fact you are living. Now we ask you and urge you in the Lord Jesus to do this more and more"* (1 Thessalonians 4:1).

▶ Classic codependent relationships are typically characterized by an emotionally *weak* person who feels the need to be connected to an emotionally *strong* person.

- The so-called *strong* one is actually *weak* because of the need to be needed.

- Both are insecure and become entangled in a web of emotional bondage.

- The two combine to produce a destructive cycle of manipulation and control, draining joy and happiness out of life.

- Because this destructive dynamic is often subconscious, both parties can feel innocent of any wrongdoing.

Yet, God knows that the self-absorbed motives of codependent people are consumed with trying to fill an empty emotional bucket that has no bottom.[11]

"All a person's ways seem pure to them,
but motives are weighed by the Lord."
(Proverbs 16:2)

CAUSES OF A VICTIM MENTALITY

Everyone who has been victimized has been overwhelmed with trauma. Many often come to distorted conclusions about themselves and their world. These incorrect beliefs lead wounded hearts to adopt faulty reactions and behaviors that hide their intense hurt and build walls that block intimacy with God.

Yet the Lord lovingly uses failures and problem relationships to reveal unresolved emotional problems. As God calls each one of us to account, His desire is to break down these dividing walls and heal hurting hearts in order to set prisoners free.

"The Spirit of the Lord is on me,
because he has anointed me to proclaim
good news to the poor.
He has sent me to proclaim freedom
for the prisoners and recovery of sight
for the blind, to set the oppressed free."
(Luke 4:18)

Unfortunately, the patterns these victims developed as children in order to survive remain part of their personalities. These patterns may become ironclad, protective walls around emotional pain or hurt, and they may keep self-awareness, vulnerability, and true intimacy in relationships at bay.

Although those who have been victimized as children yearn for mature love, often a journey back into their silenced hearts seems too threatening and the hidden deceptions too deep to understand.[12]

> "The heart is deceitful above all things and beyond cure. Who can understand it?"
> (Jeremiah 17:9)

Often those who develop a victim mentality view themselves as spiritual, emotional, and relational *prisoners of the past.*

Spiritual Prisoners of the Past

▶ **Faulty Reaction:** Blaming God

- **Distorted Conclusion:** "This is God's fault." "God is not fair!"

- **Biblical Truth:** *"He is the Rock, his works are perfect, and all his ways are just. A faithful God who does no wrong, upright and just is he"* (Deuteronomy 32:4).

▶ **Faulty Reaction:** Harboring anger toward God

- **Distorted Conclusion:** "How could God let this happen to me?" "God doesn't care about me."

- **Biblical Truth:** *"The LORD is righteous in all his ways and faithful in all he does"* (Psalm 145:17).

▶ **Faulty Reaction:** Refusing to trust God

- **Distorted Conclusion:** "I can't depend on God." "I don't believe in God."

- **Biblical Truth:** *"Trust in the LORD with all your heart and lean not on your own understanding"* (Proverbs 3:5).

▶ **Faulty Reaction:** Fearing God

- **Distorted Conclusion:** "I'm afraid of God." "I want to hide from God."

- **Biblical Truth:** *"The LORD is my light and my salvation—whom shall I fear? The Lord is the stronghold of my life—of whom shall I be afraid?"* (Psalm 27:1).

▶ **Faulty Reaction:** Doubting God's Love

- **Distorted Conclusion:** "God certainly doesn't love me." "I don't deserve God's love."

- **Biblical Truth:** *"Great is his love toward us, and the faithfulness of the Lord endures forever"* (Psalm 117:2).

Left unchecked, these spiritual walls will separate victims from the truths of Scripture, and a victim mentality will soon emerge.

Emotional Prisoners of the Past

▶ **Faulty Reaction:** Bitterness

- **Distorted Conclusion:** "I hate living in this family." "I wish I were someone else."

- **Biblical Truth:** *"See to it that no one falls short of the grace of God and that no bitter root grows up to cause trouble and defile many"* (Hebrews 12:15).

▶ **Faulty Reaction:** False Guilt

- **Distorted Conclusion:** "This is my fault." "I must not tell; I'll get in trouble."

- **Biblical Truth:** *"You desired faithfulness even in the womb; you taught me wisdom in that secret place"* (Psalm 51:6).

▶ **Faulty Reaction:** Shame

- **Distorted Conclusion:** "Something must be wrong with me." "I am a bad person."

- **Biblical Truth:** *"I praise you because I am fearfully and wonderfully made; your works are wonderful, I know that full well"* (Psalm 139:14).

▶ **Faulty Reaction:** Unforgiveness

- **Distorted Conclusion:** "I'll never forgive them." "I wish they were dead."

- **Biblical Truth:** *"If you hold anything against anyone, forgive them, so that your Father in heaven may forgive you your sins"* (Mark 11:25).

- ▶ **Faulty Reaction:** Fear

  - ▪ **Distorted Conclusion:** "What will happen to me if someone finds out?" "What if someone hurts me again?"

  - ▪ **Biblical Truth:** *"I sought the* Lord, *and he answered me; he delivered me from all my fears"* (Psalm 34:4).

- ▶ **Faulty Reaction:** Hopelessness

  - ▪ **Distorted Conclusion:** "Things have never been good." "Life will never get better."

  - ▪ **Biblical Truth:** *"I remain confident of this: I will see the goodness of the* Lord *in the land of the living"* (Psalm 27:13).

- ▶ **Faulty Reaction:** Self-centeredness

  - ▪ **Distorted Conclusion:** "I never have fun or enjoy life like others do." "It's hard to think of anything but my unhappiness."

  - ▪ **Biblical Truth:** *"The* Lord *will vindicate me; your love,* Lord, *endures forever"* (Psalm 138:8).

Left in place, these emotional walls prevent the truth of God's Word from penetrating the soul and a victim mentality takes hold.

▶ **Faulty Reaction:** Fear

- **Distorted Conclusion:** "People are unsafe." "I must protect myself."

- **Biblical Truth:** *"Do not be afraid of anyone, for judgment belongs to God"* (Deuteronomy 1:17).

▶ **Faulty Reaction:** Distrust

- **Distorted Conclusion:** "People are unreliable." "I must guard myself."

- **Biblical Truth:** *"There is a friend who sticks closer than a brother"* (Proverbs 18:24).

▶ **Faulty Reaction:** Anger

- **Distorted Conclusion:** "People are perpetrators." "I must avenge myself."

- **Biblical Truth:** *"Do not take revenge, my dear friends, but leave room for God's wrath, for it is written: 'It is mine to avenge; I will repay,' says the Lord"* (Romans 12:19).

▶ **Faulty Reaction:** Insecurity

- **Distorted Conclusion:** "People are selfish." "I must fend for myself."

- **Biblical Truth:** *"All the believers were together and had everything in common. They sold property and possessions to give to anyone who had need"* (Acts 2:44–45).

As victims of abuse move on with their lives, many outgrow their faulty and immature ways of thinking about life. They put away the past and begin to seek fulfillment through achieving personal goals, such as service to the Lord, marriage, children, career, financial success, and other personal accomplishments.

> "Do not conform to the pattern of this world, but be transformed by the renewing of your mind. Then you will be able to test and approve what God's will is— his good, pleasing and perfect will." (Romans 12:2)

WHY DOES Fostering Fearfulness Lead to a Victim Mentality?[13]

Fear does not appear "in a vacuum." Something set you up to be controlled by fear, and something serves to trigger that fear. The setup occurred in the past, while the trigger occurs in the present. Finding the truth about your fear will provide wisdom as to why you are being controlled by present fear and being held captive to a victim mentality.

> "Fear and trembling have beset me; horror has overwhelmed me." (Psalm 55:5)

Past Setups for Fear

▶ **Monumental Experiences**

- Traumatic event
- Scary situations

- Abusive relationships

- Fearful role models

Realize the reason for your fear and tell yourself the truth about the past and the present.

"When I was a child, I talked like a child, I thought like a child, I reasoned like a child. When I became a man, I put the ways of childhood behind me" (1 Corinthians 13:11).

▶ Emotional Overload

- Pent-up, unacknowledged feelings

- Unrealistic expectations

- Harsh, stressful environment

- Demanding, rejecting authority figures

Realize the reason for your fear and allow the Lord to help you heal from your hurts.

"Humble yourselves, therefore, under God's mighty hand, that he may lift you up in due time. Cast all your anxiety on him because he cares for you" (1 Peter 5:6–7).

▶ Situational Avoidance

- Refusal to face fears

- Rejection of chances for change

- Reinforcement of fears

- Repetition of negative thought patterns

Realize the reason for your fear and allow the Lord to help you face your fears.

"I am the Lord your God who takes hold of your right hand and says to you, Do not fear; I will help you" (Isaiah 41:13).

▶ **Dismal Outlook**

- Anticipation of danger and disaster

- Expectation of frustration and failure

- Belief of lies

- Rejection of truth

Realize the reason for your fear and tell yourself the truth.

"Whatever is true, whatever is noble, whatever is right, whatever is pure, whatever is lovely, whatever is admirable—if anything is excellent or praiseworthy—think about such things" (Philippians 4:8).

WHY DOES Victimization Lead to Codependency?

Just as day follows night, codependency predictably follows victimization. They tend to go hand in hand—and for good reason. Each fosters the other and imprisons victims in a repetitive, painful cycle God wants to break so that He can bring freedom.

"It is for freedom that Christ has set us free. Stand firm, then, and do not let yourselves be burdened again by a yoke of slavery." (Galatians 5:1)

QUESTION: "How are victimized children set up to become codependent adults?"

ANSWER: No one sets out to be emotionally addicted. Love cravings often are created in childhood because there is "no water in the well"—their "love buckets" are empty. These children may become adult love addicts because they ...

▶ Did not receive enough positive affirmation as children

▶ Grew up feeling unloved, insignificant, and insecure

▶ Experienced a traumatic separation or a lack of bonding

▶ Felt and continue to feel intense sadness and a profound loss at being abandoned

▶ Experienced repeated rejection from their parents

▶ Felt and continue to feel extreme fear, helplessness, and emptiness

Children with empty "love buckets" create a fantasy about some "savior" who will remove their fear and finally make them feel whole. As adults, they still behave like emotionally needy "children" who ...

▶ Believe that being loved by someone—anyone— is the solution to their emptiness

▶ Enter relationships believing the other person cannot take care of themselves

- Assign too much value and power to the other person in a relationship

- Have tremendously unrealistic expectations of the other person

- Try to "stick like glue" to the other person in order to feel connected

- Live in fear that those who truly love them will ultimately leave them

The plight of a love addict would seem without solution were it not for the Lord, who is the only true Savior, the One who loves them unconditionally and eternally. The Bible gives this assurance ...

"I have loved you with an everlasting love;
I have drawn you with unfailing kindness."
(Jeremiah 31:3)

Codependent Relationships

QUESTION: "What draws people into destructive, codependent relationships?"

ANSWER: Children who grow up being emotionally needy and who do not learn the skills necessary for forming healthy, adult relationships never learn healthy interdependence.

- They have difficulty speaking the truth, asking for what they want, and setting boundaries.

- They become codependent adults who are addicted to unhealthy relationships because they never learned anything different.

- They are desperately in need of finishing what they began early in life—to grow up emotionally, psychologically, and spiritually so they can mature relationally.

The Bible refers to immature grown-ups by using the analogy of infants feeding on milk instead of on solid food.

"Though by this time you ought to be teachers, you need someone to teach you the elementary truths of God's word all over again. You need milk, not solid food! Anyone who lives on milk, being still an infant, is not acquainted with the teaching about righteousness." (Hebrews 5:12–13)

WHAT IS the Root Cause of a Victim Mentality?

Victims who remain imprisoned by a victim mentality do so because of a belief system that keeps them locked into feeling they are powerless to change. Thus, they tend to resist accepting responsibility for personal healing and growth.

▶ **WRONG BELIEF**

"I was powerless to change my life growing up and I am powerless to change it now. What has happened to me has defined me, and I do not deserve anything better. Besides, I am not as adequate or as good as others, and the fear of being discovered as the failure I am overwhelms me."

RIGHT BELIEF

"As a child of God, I have Christ living in me, giving me His power to change. I give Him my fear of failure and accept the responsibility to overcome my past because God is faithful. He will do it! I can take my every thought captive and begin a process of reprogramming my mind so I can become emotionally, relationally, and spiritually healthy. I am determined to *'... demolish arguments and every pretension that sets itself up against the knowledge of God, and ... take captive every thought to make it obedient to Christ'* (2 Corinthians 10:5)."

"I know I can do this because *'His divine power has given* [me] *everything* [I] *need for a godly life through* [my] *knowledge of him who called* [me] *by his own glory and goodness'* (2 Peter 1:3)."

Plan of Salvation

FOUR POINTS OF GOD'S PLAN

#1 God's Purpose for You is *Salvation.*

What was God's motivation in sending Jesus Christ to earth?

To express His love for you by saving you! The Bible says, *"God so loved the world that he gave his one and only Son, that whoever believes in him shall not perish but have eternal life. For God did not send his Son into the world to condemn the world, but to save the world through him"* (John 3:16–17).

To forgive your sins, to empower you to have victory over sin, and to enable you to live a fulfilled life! Jesus said, *"I have come that they may have life, and that they may have it more abundantly"* (John 10:10 NKJV).

#2 Your Problem is *Sin*.

Sin is living independently of God's standard—knowing what is right, but choosing what is wrong. The Bible says, *"If anyone, then, knows the good they ought to do and doesn't do it, it is sin for them"* (James 4:17).

Spiritual death, eternal separation from God. Scripture states, *"Your iniquities* [sins] *have separated you from your God"* (Isaiah 59:2). *"The wages of sin is death, but the gift of God is eternal life in Christ Jesus our Lord"* (Romans 6:23).

#3 God's Provision for You is the *Savior*.

Yes! Jesus died on the cross to personally pay the penalty for your sins. The Bible says, *"God demonstrates his own love for us in this: While we were still sinners, Christ died for us"* (Romans 5:8).

What is the solution to being separated from God?

Belief in (entrusting your life to) Jesus Christ as the only way to God the Father. Jesus says, *"I am the way and the truth and the life. No one comes to the Father except through me"* (John 14:6). *"Believe in the Lord Jesus, and you will be saved"* (Acts 16:31).

#4 Your Part is *Surrender.*

Give Christ control of your life, entrusting yourself to Him.

"Jesus said to his disciples, 'Whoever wants to be my disciple must deny themselves and take up their cross [die to your own self-rule] and follow me. For whoever wants to save their life will lose it, but whoever loses their life for me will find it. What good will it be for someone to gain the whole world, yet forfeit their soul?'" (Matthew 16:24–26).

Place your faith in (rely on) Jesus Christ as your personal Lord and Savior and reject your "good works" as a means of earning God's approval. *"It is by grace you have been saved, through faith— and this is not from yourselves, it is the gift of God—not by works, so that no one can boast"* (Ephesians 2:8–9).

The moment you choose to receive Jesus as your Lord and Savior—entrusting your life to Him—He comes to live inside you. Then He gives you His power to live the fulfilled life God has planned for you. If you want to be fully forgiven by God and become the person God created you to be, you can tell Him in a simple, heartfelt prayer like this:

PRAYER OF SALVATION

*"God, I want a real relationship with You.
I admit that many times I've chosen
to go my own way instead of Your way.
Please forgive me for my sins.
Jesus, thank You for dying on the cross to
pay the penalty for my sins.
Come into my life to be
my Lord and my Savior.
Change me from the inside out and make
me the person You created me to be.
In Your holy name I pray. Amen."*

WHAT CAN YOU NOW EXPECT?

If you sincerely prayed this prayer, look at what God says about you!

"Since we have been justified through faith,
we have peace with God
through our Lord Jesus Christ,
through whom we have gained access by
faith into this grace in which we now stand.
And we boast in the hope
of the glory of God."
(Romans 5:1–2)

STEPS TO SOLUTION

Apart from the supernatural work of the Spirit of God within the lives of victims, there is no solid solution to the serious side effects of being victimized.

Such a work is based on having a personal relationship with God, on seeing Him as He really is—a gracious and compassionate heavenly Father, full of tender mercies. This requires replacing distorted images of God with the truth about His character. It requires maturing in the Lord, walking with Him on a daily basis, confiding in Him, and learning to trust Him for life itself.

Understanding the life-changing effects of being victimized by others is not for the purpose of placing blame, becoming bitter, or for excusing our failures. It is accepting the fact that facing ourselves is necessary for identifying and replacing past problematic programming with the transforming Word of God.

"For the word of God is alive and active.
Sharper than any double-edged sword,
it penetrates even to dividing soul and spirit,
joints and marrow; it judges the thoughts
and attitudes of the heart."
(Hebrews 4:12)

Key Passage to Read

READ PSALM 91

"He will command his angels concerning
you to guard you in all your ways."
(Psalm 91:11)

His guardian angels have watchcare over you.

▶ Rest in the presence of Almighty God. (v. 1)

▶ Trust in the defense of your loving God. (v. 2)

▶ Believe in the faithfulness of your God. (vv. 3–7)

▶ See your vindication as coming from God. (v. 8)

▶ Live in the safety of your sheltering God. (vv. 9–10)

▶ Know you are guarded by angels sent from God. (vv. 11–13)

▶ Rely on the protection of your loving God. (v. 14)

▶ Call on your Savior and God for deliverance. (vv. 15–16)

Uncovering buried feelings from your past can be painful. Therefore, it can seem easier to stay angry than to understand the cause, turn loose of your "rights," and grow in maturity.[14] The Bible gives specific, practical solutions in the form of three "do nots."

> "'In your anger do not sin': Do not let the sun go down while you are still angry, and do not give the devil a foothold." (Ephesians 4:26–27)

One of the first steps toward overcoming a victim mentality is looking at your present anger patterns and the picture they paint of your past victimizations. Learning the cause of your anger will aid you in learning to resolve your anger.

The Four Causes of Anger

1 Hurt[15]—Your heart is wounded.

Everyone has a God-given inner need for unconditional love.[16] When you experience rejection or emotional pain of any kind, anger can become a protective wall that keeps people and pain away.

2 Injustice[17]—Your right is violated.

Everyone has an inner moral code that produces a sense of right and wrong, fair and unfair, just and unjust. When you perceive that an injustice has occurred against you or others (especially those whom you love), you may feel angry. If you hold on to the offense, the unresolved anger can begin to make a home in your heart.

3 Fear[18] —Your future is threatened.

Everyone is created with a God-given inner need for security.[19] When you begin to worry, feel threatened, or get angry because of a change in circumstances, you may be responding to fear. A fearful heart reveals a lack of trust in God's perfect plan for your life.

4 Frustration[20]—Your performance is not accepted.

Everyone has a God-given inner need for significance.[21] When your efforts are thwarted or do not meet your own personal expectations, your sense of significance can be threatened. Frustration over unmet expectations of yourself or of others is a major source of anger.

> " ... human anger does not produce the righteousness that God desires."
> (James 1:20)

In searching your heart, decide that you will not allow anger to dictate your decisions or control your emotions. Instead, turn your hurts, rights, fears, and frustrations over to God and enter into a deeper dependence on Him to meet your God-given needs.

Remember ...

"The LORD will guide you always;
he will satisfy your needs in a sun-scorched
land and will strengthen your frame.
You will be like a well-watered garden,
like a spring whose waters never fail."
(Isaiah 58:11)

HOW TO Free Yourself from Unresolved Anger

Many of us assume that once we reach adulthood, our pain from childhood will just disappear and no longer affect us. But this disappearing act does not happen unless we identify our past pains from childhood and resolve them. While we are not the sum of our experiences, we are shaped by our responses to our experiences.

God does not want us to store the bad things that happened to us by stockpiling our anger. Rather, He wants us to be like a storehouse where we get rid of the bad fruit of anger, resentment, distrust, and fearfulness and store up the good fruit of joy, peace, patience, kindness, and all the good fruit of forgiveness.

"A good man brings good things
out of the good stored up in him,
and an evil man brings evil things
out of the evil stored up in him."
(Matthew 12:35)

Resolving Anger Rooted in Childhood Victimizations

The next time anger wells up in your heart or uncontrollable tears stream down your face, ask yourself ...

▶ What am I feeling: hurt, injustice, fear, or frustration?

▶ Did I have any of these same feelings when I was a child?

Face your anger from the past and begin to see how your present anger is connected to your unresolved childhood anger.

▶ Ask God to reveal buried hurts, injustices, fears, and frustrations from your childhood.

▶ Take four pieces of paper and label one "Hurt," one "Injustice," one "Fear," and one "Frustration." Then write down every instance of each you can remember from your life.

Release your anger over each instance to God and replace the anger with God's peace.

▶ Forgive and pray for those toward whom you have harbored anger.

▶ Burn the pages as a personal, symbolic reminder of your forgiveness.

Ask God to reveal the relationship between your past and present anger.

▶ Ask close family and friends what makes you angry and how they know when you are angry.

▶ Ask forgiveness from anyone you have offended by your anger.

Assume personal responsibility for your present feelings of anger.

▶ Meditate on how God has demonstrated His great love for you.

▶ If your heart yearns for love and acceptance, remember, *"This is how God showed his love among us: He sent his one and only Son into the world that we might live through him. This is love: not that we loved God, but that he loved us and sent his Son as an atoning sacrifice for our sins"* (1 John 4:9–10).

HOW TO Find Freedom from the Victim Mentality

Finding freedom is a process that takes time and has periods of regression. You may have seasons when it seems no progress is being made at all. The first step in the process is deciding that you want to heal and believing that healing is possible with God. As you place your hope in Him and seek His plan for you, wait patiently for the Lord to lovingly show you the way.

"No one who hopes in you will ever be put to shame, but shame will come on those who are treacherous without cause. Show me your ways, LORD, teach me your paths" (Psalm 25:3–4).

QUESTION: "How can I be healed?"

ANSWER: You can be healed through the power of the Lord. It will take time, but healing can occur through a positive process in which you will experience spiritual growth.

> "Heal me, LORD, and I will be healed;
> save me and I will be saved,
> for you are the one I praise."
> (Jeremiah 17:14)

Healing does not come instantaneously, but is a process that includes the following steps:

1. Accept that pain is a part of this life, common to everyone, and you are one among many victims (John 16:33).

2. Begin to see your life from God's perspective—He is in control and wants to bless you and conform you to the image of His Son, Jesus (Ephesians 4:22–24).

3. Seek appropriate help from those whom you trust—those who are spiritually and emotionally mature and skilled enough to help you (Proverbs 10:17).

4. Learn to relax and allow yourself time to meaningfully connect with God and other significant persons (Philippians 4:6; Hebrews 10:25).

5. Believe in and trust in the promises of God's Word. Allow His Word to "reprogram" your thought processes so that you will be able to replace the lies of your past with His eternal truth (Colossians 3:10–14).

The Bible says ...

> "My comfort in my suffering is this:
> Your promise preserves my life."
> (Psalm 119:50)

As you begin the process of healing and finding freedom from your bondage to victimization, there are several painful realities you will need to face and work through.

Face Your Prison

▶ Recognizing your prison walls is necessary in order to tear down those walls and experience the total freedom God plans for you. Ask yourself ...

☐ Do I feel there is no way out of my situation?

☐ Do I think love is based on my performance?

☐ Do I feel powerless in my relationships?

☐ Do I lie in order to avoid conflict?

☐ Do I think other people are better than me?

☐ Do I have a lack of trust in people?

☐ Do I have difficulty saying *no*?

☐ Do I fear rejection?

▶ Acknowledging your bondage and your need to break through the walls that are keeping you from having healthy relationships is critical to the healing process.

- Acknowledge your bondage by confessing it to God.

- Acknowledge your realization that your bondage has hindered both your relationship with God and your relationships with others.

- Acknowledge your need for God's divine intervention in your life.

- Acknowledge your dependence on Him to empower you to walk in freedom.

- Acknowledge your need for a new way of thinking about Him, yourself, and others.

- Acknowledge your need to see yourself from God's viewpoint.

- Acknowledge your need to understand what constitutes a healthy relationship from God's perspective.

- Acknowledge your bondage by sharing it with one or two trusted confidants who will agree to hold you accountable to work toward becoming mature in Christ.

Remember the admonition in God's Word that we are to *"carry each other's burdens, and in this way you will fulfill the law of Christ"* (Galatians 6:2).

▶ Remembering past victimization is sometimes the first step toward healing.

To induce memory, God often uses ...

- Flashbacks
- Parenthood
- Media coverage
- Victory over an addiction
- Dreams and nightmares
- A significant death
- Touch
- Testimony of others

▶ Journaling can help you to move through the stages of remembering.

Writing down your thoughts and feelings helps you ...

- Face the fact of the abuse
- Recall the feelings associated with the abuse
- Uncover hidden fury associated with the abuse
- Process your feelings about the abuse
- Objectify the abuse
- Organize the events surrounding the abuse
- Discover the ramifications of the abuse
- Gain insights into any present abuse

Memorize this passage: *"I have been deprived of peace; I have forgotten what prosperity is. So I say, 'My splendor is gone and all that I had hoped from the Lord.' I remember my affliction and my wandering, the bitterness and the gall. I well remember them, and my soul is downcast within me. Yet this I call to mind and therefore I have hope: Because of the Lord's great love we are not consumed, for his compassions never fail"* (Lamentations 3:17–22).

Face Your Patterns of Behavior[23]

▶ Realizing what you are doing to get your inner needs met can provide meaningful insight. Ask yourself ...

☐ Am I compromising my values in order to feel loved?

☐ Am I violating my conscience in order to feel secure?

☐ Am I being a perfectionist, a workaholic, a fixer in order to feel significant?

☐ Am I cycling through one idolatrous, codependent relationship after another in a vain attempt to fill my "love bucket"?

Remember, *"No temptation has overtaken you except what is common to mankind. And God is faithful; he will not let you be tempted beyond what you can bear. But when you are tempted, he will also provide a way out so that you can endure it"* (1 Corinthians 10:13).

Face Your Private Secret[24]

▶ Understanding the bondage secrets create is essential to breaking down prison walls.

- Talking about the past brings it into reality.

- Telling someone else gives your past credibility.

- Telling the secret breaks its power over you.

- Telling brings what was done in the dark out into the light for healing.

Scripture reminds us, *"Therefore confess your sins to each other and pray for each other so that you may be healed. The prayer of a righteous person is powerful and effective"* (James 5:16).

Face Your Pain[25]

▶ Walking through the emotional pain of victimization is one of the most difficult but most necessary steps in breaking down the walls that keep you in bondage.

- Pain confirms your abuse.

- Pain unacknowledged is pain unhealed.

- Pain expressed is often pain released.

- Pain is unpleasant but not unbearable.

Be assured, *"If we confess our sins, he is faithful and just and will forgive us our sins and purify us from all unrighteousness"* (1 John 1:9).

Face Your Victimizer—If It Is Safe[26]

▶ Standing up for yourself and taking back control over your life—and your body—is liberating in itself.

- Pray for God's timing and the preparation of your heart and the heart of the victimizer.

- Identify realistic goals that you hope to accomplish through the confrontation.

- Write down what you plan to say and rehearse it with someone beforehand.

- Be prepared for the offender to deny having abused you.

- When the time is appropriate, talk with your perpetrator one on one, or take someone you trust with you if you think it is necessary.

- Let go of secret hopes and expectations—just know that your confrontation is biblical.

"If your brother or sister sins, go and point out their fault." (Matthew 18:15)

Face Your Pardon[27]

▶ Learning the truth about guilt and forgiveness is a major key to living in freedom.

- Forgive yourself.

- Forgive the offender.

- Forgive anyone who has overtly or covertly victimized you.

- Forgiveness gives you freedom by taking vengeance out of your hands and putting it in God's hands to avenge.[28]

> "For we know him who said,
> 'It is mine to avenge; I will repay,' and again,
> 'The Lord will judge his people.'"
> (Hebrews 10:30)

Face Your Predicament[29]

▶ Knowing that God permitted your victimization but in no way caused it or condoned it is paramount! God hates evil and violence and will one day totally obliterate all evil and evil practices. He will pronounce eternal judgment on all who persist in their evil ways.

> "I will punish the world for its evil, the wicked for their sins. I will put an end to the arrogance of the haughty and will humble the pride of the ruthless." (Isaiah 13:11)

HOW TO Forgive Your Victimizer

Have you ever noticed that the word *forgiveness* has the little word *give* in it? When you choose to forgive, you give someone a gift of freedom from having to pay the penalty for offending you—the gift of dismissing the debt owed to you! Because this can be a difficult gift to give, you may need to travel through four stages of forgiveness. But realize that you are also giving yourself a gift of grudge-free living. That is true freedom. And that is why the Bible says ...

> "Do not seek revenge or bear a grudge against anyone among your people, but love your neighbor as yourself."
> (Leviticus 19:18)

The Four Stages of Forgiveness

1 Face the Offense.

When you feel pain that is personal, unfair, and deep, you have a wound that can be healed only by forgiving the one who wounded you. First, you must face the truth of what has actually been done and not hinder true healing by rationalizing and focusing on false thinking.

> "Be kind and compassionate to one another, forgiving each other, just as in Christ God forgave you." (Ephesians 4:32)

▶ Don't minimize the offense by thinking: "No matter how badly he treats me, it's okay."

TRUTH: Bad treatment is not okay. There is no excuse for bad treatment of any kind—anytime.

"Have nothing to do with the fruitless deeds of darkness, but rather expose them" (Ephesians 5:11).

▶ Don't excuse the offender's behavior by thinking: "He doesn't mean to hurt me. I shouldn't feel upset with him—he's a member of my family!"

TRUTH: No matter the age of the offender or our relationship, we need to call sin "sin." We need to face the truth instead of trying to change it. There must first be a guilty party in order to have someone to forgive.

"Whoever says to the guilty, 'You are innocent,' will be cursed by peoples" (Proverbs 24:24).

▶ Don't assume that quick forgiveness is full forgiveness by thinking:[30] "As soon as that horrendous ordeal occurred, I quickly and fully forgave him. That's what I've been taught to do!"

TRUTH: Many well-intentioned people feel guilty if they don't extend immediate forgiveness. As a result, they "forgive" quickly. Yet they have neither faced the full impact of the offense nor grieved over what actually happened. Rarely is the full impact of sin felt at the moment it occurs. Rather, its impact is felt at different levels over a period of time.

Therefore, forgiveness needs to be extended at each of these levels. "Quick forgiveness" over deep hurts may seem sufficient, but it is not "full forgiveness"—not until it has been extended at each level of impact. Before complete forgiveness can be extended, you must face the truth about the gravity of the offense and its extended impact on you.

"You [God] desired faithfulness
even in the womb; you taught me wisdom
in that secret place."
(Psalm 51:6)

2 Feel the Offense.[31]

We usually do not hate strangers or acquaintances; we just "get angry" with strangers. But Lewis Smedes writes, "When a person destroys what our commitment and our intimacy created, something precious is destroyed."[32] Then anger or even hatred may be our true feelings in response to deep, unfair pain. Hatred toward an offender needs to be brought up out of the basement of our souls and dealt with. However, not all hatred is wrong. God hates evil.

"But you, Sovereign Lord, help me for your name's sake; out of the goodness of your love, deliver me. For I am poor and needy, and my heart is wounded within me."
(Psalm 109:21–22)

▶ Don't deny your pain by thinking: "I don't blame her for always criticizing me. She is under a lot of pressure—and it doesn't hurt me."

TRUTH: Being mistreated by someone you love is painful. Feeling the pain must take place before healing can take place.

"The Lord is close to the broken hearted and saves those who are crushed in spirit" (Psalm 34:18).

▶ Don't carry false guilt by thinking: "I feel guilty if I hate what was done to me. I'm never supposed to have hatred."

TRUTH: God hates sin. You too can hate sin. You are to hate the sin, but not the sinner.

"To fear the Lord *is to hate evil; I hate pride and arrogance, evil behavior and perverse speech"* (Proverbs 8:13).

3 Forgive the Offender.

"To err is human, to forgive, divine."[33] This famous quote by Alexander Pope is a heavenly reminder to all of us. However, the earthly reality is more like this: "To err is human, to blame it on someone else is more human!" Oh, how much easier it is to blame than to forgive. But we are called by God to forgive. And when you do forgive, genuine forgiveness draws you into the heart of God, and your life takes on the divine character of Christ.

> "You show that you are a letter from Christ, the result of our ministry,
> written not with ink but with the Spirit of the living God, not on tablets of stone but on tablets of human hearts."
> (2 Corinthians 3:3)

▶ Make a list of all the offenses caused by your offender.

▶ Imagine right now that a hook is attached to your collarbone. And imagine attached to the hook all the pain resulting from the wrong that was done to you.

▶ Ask yourself, *Do I really want to carry all that pain with me for the rest of my life?* The Lord wants you to take the pain from the past and release it into His hands.

▶ Then take the one who offended you off of your emotional hook and place your offender onto God's hook. The Lord knows how to deal with your offender in His time and in His way. God says, *"Bear with each other and forgive one another, if any of you has a grievance against someone. Forgive as the Lord forgave you"* (Colossians 3:13).

PRAYER TO FORGIVE YOUR OFFENDER

"Lord Jesus, thank You for caring about how much my heart has been hurt. You know the pain I have felt because of (list every offense). Right now I release all that pain into Your hands. Thank You, Jesus, for dying on the cross for me and extending Your forgiveness to me. As an act of my will, I choose to forgive (name). Right now, I move (name) off of my emotional hook to Your hook. I refuse all thoughts of revenge. I trust that in Your time and in Your way You will deal with my offender as You see fit. And Lord, thank You for giving me Your power to forgive so that I can be set free. In Your holy name I pray. Amen."

4 Find Oneness.

Relationships filled with resentment ultimately perish—relationships filled with forgiveness ultimately prevail. However, reconciliation in a relationship—the restoration of oneness—is contingent on several vital factors, with the primary one being that the offender confess, repent, and demonstrate a changed life. When these conditions are met, when both parties are committed to conformity to Christ and honesty in the relationship, there is real hope that the two can be of one mind and one heart again.[34]

The Bible says ...

> "If you have any encouragement from being
> united with Christ, if any comfort from his
> love, if any common sharing in the Spirit,
> if any tenderness and compassion,
> then make my joy complete by being like-
> minded, having the same love,
> being one in spirit and of one mind."
> (Philippians 2:1–2)

QUESTION: "How can I release the bitterness I feel toward my victimizer who is now dead?"

ANSWER: Although you cannot confront your victimizer in person, you can confront indirectly by saying what you would want to say or need to say as though your offender is in front of you.

▶ Consider the "chair technique." Imagine the person seated in a chair placed in front of you. Say the things you would say to the person if you were actually seated across a table from one another. Express your feelings about what was done to you and the ramifications those events have had on your life. Then forgive the person and explain that you have taken the person off of your emotional hook and placed the person onto God's hook.

▶ Write a letter to your victimizer, stating every painful memory. Read it over the person's grave or at a place where you can openly speak to the person as though you were in each other's presence. Then at the close, choose to forgive by releasing your victimizer into the hands of God.

▶ Make a list of all painful as well as positive memories. After completing the list, go back to the beginning and write the word "past" by each memory. Acknowledge and accept that the past is in the past. As an act of your will, release all the pain as well as the person into the hands of God. Take the person and the pain off of your emotional hook and put them onto God's hook.

The fact that your victimizer has died does not mean that you cannot forgive and thereby prevent bitterness from establishing a foothold in your heart and mind.

The Bible says ...

"See to it that no one falls short of the grace of God and that no bitter root grows up to cause trouble and defile many."
(Hebrews 12:15)

Victimization and rejection are constant companions and construct strong prison walls around the hearts of many victims. The messages they relay to their captives are bitterly painful and terribly destructive. The lies they convey must be countered with the truth of Scripture.

> "You desired faithfulness even in the womb; you taught me wisdom in that secret place." (Psalm 51:6)

When you experience ...

▶ **Rejection**

- Tell yourself the truth, "Just because someone withholds love from me doesn't mean everyone will withhold love from me. God will always listen to me and will never withhold His love from me."

"Praise be to God, who has not rejected my prayer or withheld his love from me!" (Psalm 66:20).

▶ **Worthlessness**

- Tell yourself the truth, "Just because someone doesn't value me doesn't mean no one values me. God values me enough to send Jesus to die for me so that I can spend eternity with Him!"

"This is how God showed his love among us: He sent his one and only Son into the world that we might live through him" (1 John 4:9).

▶ Self-hate

- Tell yourself the truth, "Just because someone has judged and condemned me doesn't mean I should condemn myself. God will never condemn me, because I am set free in Christ."

"Therefore, there is now no condemnation for those who are in Christ Jesus, because through Christ Jesus the law of the Spirit who gives life has set you free from the law of sin and death" (Romans 8:1–2).

In order to break the cycle of rejection in your life, focus on facts, not on feelings. The fact is you are ACCEPTED.

A —**ADMIT** the rejection of the past and acknowledge its pain.

C —**CLAIM** God's acceptance and unconditional love.

C —**CHOOSE** to forgive those who rejected you.

E —**EXPECT** future rejection to be natural in a fallen world.

P —**PLANT** Scripture in your mind to produce new and truthful thought patterns.

T —**THANK** God for what you've learned through your rejection.

E —**ENCOURAGE** others as an expression of Christ's love.

D —**DRAW** on the power of Christ's life within you.

"You, dear children, are from God and have overcome them, because the one who is in you is greater than the one who is in the world." (1 John 4:4)

▶ Remember ...

- Jesus knew to expect unjustified hatred—and He tells you to expect unjustified hatred.

  "I have chosen you out of the world. That is why the world hates you" (John 15:19).

- Jesus knew to expect persecution—and He tells you to expect persecution.

  "If they persecuted me, they will persecute you also" (John 15:20).

- Jesus had enemies, yet He loved them—and He tells you to love your enemies and do good to them.

  "Love your enemies, do good to them ... " (Luke 6:35).

- Jesus prayed for those who persecuted Him— and He tells you to pray for your persecutors.

  "Pray for those who persecute you ... " (Matthew 5:44).

- Jesus modeled forgiveness toward those who sinned against Him—and He tells you to forgive those who sin against you.

  "If you forgive other people when they sin against you, your heavenly Father will also forgive you" (Matthew 6:14).

- Jesus understood that those rejecting Him were really rejecting His Father—and He tells you that those rejecting you are really rejecting Him.

  " *... whoever rejects you rejects me ...* " (Luke 10:16).

- Jesus said He would be rejected, but in the end there would be blessing—and He tells you that you will be rejected, but in the end there will be blessing.

  "Blessed are you when people hate you, when they exclude you and insult you and reject your name as evil, because of the Son of Man" (Luke 6:22).

- Jesus expected trouble as He submitted to the Father's purpose—yet Jesus was an overcomer! And He tells you to expect trouble, but when trouble comes, if you will submit to the Father's purpose, you'll be an overcomer!

  "Everyone born of God overcomes the world. This is the victory that has overcome the world, even our faith" (1 John 5:4).

HOW TO Conquer Irrational Fear

The love of God is the antidote for fear. The presence of overwhelming fear is the absence of confidence in the character of the God of the Bible and the assurance of His love for you. If your perception is that God is not "for you," then you have only your own resources on which to rely and your own philosophy about life to comfort and sustain you. How you respond to fear is often directly related to what you believe about God and what you believe about His promises regarding you and your life.

The truth is ...

> "The LORD is trustworthy
> in all he promises
> and faithful in all he does."
> (Psalm 145:13)

When you feel afraid of a person or a situation ...

▶ Ask yourself whether what you are afraid of is actually going to happen.

▶ Assess whether what you fear is something that is even likely to happen.

▶ Realize that fixating on your fear guarantees its repetition.

▶ Understand that most fears have nothing to do with what's happening.

▶ Identify the past trauma(s) that first instilled your fear.

- ▶ Determine how current the fear is that you are presently feeling. Ask yourself ...

  - "What past fear am I bringing into the present?"

  - "When did this fear first begin?"

  - "How old do I feel emotionally when I feel this fear?"

  - "Where am I when I feel this fear?"

  - "What is going on when I feel this fear?"

  - "How is this fear affecting my life now? What is it costing me?"

- ▶ Tell yourself, "I will not let this fear run my life. I will not let past or present fears control me."

- ▶ Repeat this phrase over and over, "That was then, and this is now. That was then, and this is now."

- ▶ Determine to get out of the grip of fear.

- ▶ Do what it takes to control your fear and to change from being fearful to being confident and peaceful.

- ▶ Decide to live in the here and now and act in a way that is not based on fear.

- ▶ Share your fear and your plan for change with a trustworthy person who will keep you accountable.

"The LORD himself goes before you and will be with you; he will never leave you nor forsake you. Do not be afraid; do not be discouraged." (Deuteronomy 31:8)

For Christians to walk in victory, we need to identify the lies we believe about ourselves and exchange them for the truth about who we really are in Christ. For lasting change to occur, we must cast aside the lies and constantly rely on the truth of Scripture.

"[You] were taught in him in accordance with the truth that is in Jesus. You were taught, with regard to your former way of life, to put off your old self ... to be made new in the attitude of your minds; and to put on the new self, created to be like God in true righteousness and holiness."
(Ephesians 4:21–24)

▶ **I am chosen by God.**

"He chose us in him before the creation of the world to be holy and blameless in his sight" (Ephesians 1:4).

▶ **I am adopted by God.**

"In love he predestined us for adoption to sonship through Jesus Christ, in accordance with his pleasure and will ... " (Ephesians 1:4–5).

▶ **I am a child of God.**

"To all who did receive him, to those who believed in his name, he gave the right to become children of God ... " (John 1:12).

▶ I am born again.

"You have been born again, not of perishable seed, but of imperishable, through the living and enduring word of God" (1 Peter 1:23).

▶ I am a new creation.

"If anyone is in Christ, the new creation has come: The old has gone, the new is here!" (2 Corinthians 5:17).

▶ I have a new nature.

"In him you were also circumcised with a circumcision not performed by human hands. Your whole self ruled by the flesh was put off when you were circumcised by Christ ... " (Colossians 2:11).

▶ I have a new heart.

"I will give you a new heart and put a new spirit in you; I will remove from you your heart of stone and give you a heart of flesh" (Ezekiel 36:26).

▶ I have a new spirit.

"I will put my Spirit in you and move you to follow my decrees and be careful to keep my laws" (Ezekiel 36:27).

▶ I have a new mind.

"'Who has known the mind of the Lord so as to instruct him?' But we have the mind of Christ" (1 Corinthians 2:16).

▶ I am clothed with Christ.

"All of you who were baptized into Christ have clothed yourselves with Christ" (Galatians 3:27).

▶ I am baptized into Christ.

"We were therefore buried with him through baptism into death in order that, just as Christ was raised from the dead through the glory of the Father, we too may live a new life" (Romans 6:4).

▶ I am hidden in Christ.

"You died, and your life is now hidden with Christ in God" (Colossians 3:3).

▶ I am sealed with the Spirit of Christ.

"You also were included in Christ when you heard the message of truth, the gospel of your salvation. When you believed, you were marked in him with a seal, the promised Holy Spirit, who is a deposit guaranteeing our inheritance until the redemption of those who are God's possession—to the praise of his glory" (Ephesians 1:13–14).

▶ I am redeemed.

"In him we have redemption through his blood, the forgiveness of sins, in accordance with the riches of God's grace ... " (Ephesians 1:7).

▶ I am washed.

"That is what some of you were [wicked]. But you were washed, you were sanctified, you were justified in the name of the Lord Jesus Christ and by the Spirit of our God" (1 Corinthians 6:11).

▶ I am purified.

"If we walk in the light, as he is in the light, we have fellowship with one another, and the blood of Jesus, his Son, purifies us from all sin" (1 John 1:7).

▶ I am justified.

"Since we have been justified through faith, we have peace with God through our Lord Jesus Christ ... " (Romans 5:1).

▶ I am totally accepted by Christ.

"Accept one another, then, just as Christ accepted you, in order to bring praise to God" (Romans 15:7).

▶ I am totally blameless before Christ.

"For he chose us in him before the creation of the world to be holy and blameless in his sight" (Ephesians 1:4).

▶ I am totally righteous in Christ.

"God made him who had no sin to be sin for us, so that in him we might become the righteousness of God" (2 Corinthians 5:21).

▶ I am totally complete in Christ.

"In Christ all the fullness of the Deity lives in bodily form, and in Christ you have been brought to fullness [made complete]. He is the head over every power and authority" (Colossians 2:9–10).

▶ I am totally perfect in Christ.

"By one sacrifice he has made perfect forever those who are being made holy" (Hebrews 10:14).

▶ I am free from accusation.

"He has reconciled you by Christ's physical body through death to present you holy in his sight, without blemish and free from accusation ... " (Colossians 1:22).

▶ I am free from condemnation.

"There is now no condemnation for those who are in Christ Jesus ..." (Romans 8:1).

▶ I am free from the law.

"My brothers and sisters, you also died to the law through the body of Christ, that you might belong to another, to him who was raised from the dead, in order that we might bear fruit for God" (Romans 7:4).

▶ I am free from God's wrath.

"Since we have now been justified by his blood, how much more shall we be saved from God's wrath through him!" (Romans 5:9).

▶ I have been made an heir of God.

"You are no longer a slave, but God's child; and since you are his child, God has made you also an heir" (Galatians 4:7).

▶ I have inherited everything I need to be godly.

"His divine power has given us everything we need for a godly life through our knowledge of him who called us by his own glory and goodness" (2 Peter 1:3).

▶ **I have inherited a new nature in Christ.**

"Through these he has given us his very great and precious promises, so that through them you may participate in the divine nature, having escaped the corruption in the world caused by evil desires" (2 Peter 1:4).

▶ **I have inherited every spiritual blessing.**

"Praise be to the God and Father of our Lord Jesus Christ, who has blessed us in the heavenly realms with every spiritual blessing in Christ" (Ephesians 1:3).

▶ **I have inherited eternal life.**

"This is the testimony: God has given us eternal life, and this life is in his Son" (1 John 5:11).

HOW TO Know Your Real Self-Worth

Victimization sabotages the self-worth of its victims. To be devalued by another person can leave lasting scars and sends a strong message that the victim has little or no worth. Such lies are clearly countered by the words of Jesus.

"Look at the birds of the air; they do not sow or reap or store away in barns, and yet your heavenly Father feeds them. Are you not much more valuable than they?"
(Matthew 6:26)

If you are struggling with your worth and value to God, memorize **Psalm 139**.

▶ Realize that God knows all about you! (vv. 1–6)

▶ Remember that God is always with you! (vv. 7–12)

▶ Respect the fact that God created you! (vv. 13–14)

▶ Recognize that God uniquely designed you! (vv. 15–16)

▶ Receive God's loving thoughts toward you! (vv. 17–18)

▶ Renounce God's enemies as enemies to you! (vv. 19–22)

▶ Respond to God's changing work within you! (vv. 23–24)

As you meditate on Psalm 139, accept the truth that you are …

WORTHY

W —**WORK** on eliminating negative attitudes and beliefs.

O —**OBTAIN** a scriptural understanding of having love for yourself.

R —**REFUSE** to compare yourself with others.

T —**THANK** God for His unconditional love for you.

H —**HOPE** in God's promise to mold you to be like Christ.

Y —**YIELD** your talents and abilities to helping others.

When you were a child, you did not have control over those in authority over you, but that is no longer the case. You are now able to choose those with whom you associate, and you can certainly control your self-talk. Therefore, you can take an active part in replacing the distorted view you have of yourself with God's view of you. And you can begin by starting to ...

▶ **Accept yourself.**

- Stop striving for perfection or to be like someone else.

- Realize, the Lord made you for a purpose. He designed your personality and gave you the gifts and abilities He wanted you to have in order to accomplish His purpose for you.

"Many are the plans in a person's heart, but it is the Lord's purpose that prevails" (Proverbs 19:21).

▶ **Thank God for encouraging you.**

- Acknowledge and praise God for the abilities He has given you and the things He has accomplished through you.

- Engage in biblically-based, encouraging self-talk. Mute the condemning critic inside your head.

"May our Lord Jesus Christ himself and God our Father, who loved us and by his grace gave us eternal encouragement and good hope, encourage your hearts and strengthen you in every good deed and word" (2 Thessalonians 2:16–17).

▶ **Accept the compliments of others.**

- To discount the positive comments of those who have heartfelt appreciation for you is to discount their opinions and their desire to express their gratitude to you.

- Practice graciously accepting compliments and turning them into praise to God for the affirmation that He is at work in you and producing good "fruit" through you.

"This is to my Father's glory, that you bear much fruit, showing yourselves to be my disciples" (John 15:8).

▶ **Release past negative experiences and focus on a positive future.**

- Refuse to dwell on negative things said or done to you in the past. Release them to God.

- Embrace the work God is doing in your life now and cooperate with Him by dwelling on Him, His character, and His promises to you to fulfill His purposes in you.

"It is God who works in you to will and to act in order to fulfill his good purpose" (Philippians 2:13).

▶ **Live in God's forgiveness.**

- God has extended forgiveness to you for all of your sins (past, present, and future), so confess and repent of anything offensive to God. Do not set yourself up as a higher judge than God by refusing to forgive yourself.

- Lay harsh judgment of yourself aside and accept that you will not be made "fully perfect" and totally without sin until you stand in the presence of Christ and are fully conformed to His image.

"Dear friends, now we are children of God, and what we will be has not yet been made known. But we know that when Christ appears, we shall be like him, for we shall see him as he is. All who have this hope in him purify themselves, just as he is pure" (1 John 3:2–3).

▶ **Benefit from mistakes.**

- Realize that you can learn from your mistakes as well as from the mistakes of others. Decide to view your mistakes as opportunities to learn needed lessons.

- Ask God what He wants to teach you from your mistakes; listen to Him and learn. Then move forward with a positive attitude and put into practice the insights you have gained.

"'My [Jesus'] *grace is sufficient for you, for my power is made perfect in weakness.' Therefore I* [Paul] *will boast all the more gladly about my weaknesses, so that Christ's power may rest on me"* (2 Corinthians 12:9).

▶ **Form supportive, positive relationships.**

- Realize that critical people are hurt people who project their own feelings of inadequacy onto others in an attempt to ease their own emotional pain.

- Minimize the time you spend with negative, critical people, whether family, friends, or coworkers. Seek out those who encourage and support you both emotionally and spiritually.

"Walk with the wise and become wise, for a companion of fools suffers harm" (Proverbs 13:20).

▶ **Formulate realistic goals and plans.**

- Elicit the help of others to identify your strengths and weaknesses. Discover the gifts God has given you, plus the things you are persuaded God has called you to do.

- Prayerfully set some reasonable, achievable goals that capitalize on your strengths. Make a plan for how you will set about to accomplish those goals.

"Do you not know that in a race all the runners run, but only one gets the prize? Run in such a way as to get the prize" (1 Corinthians 9:24).

▶ **Identify your heart's desires.**

- Make a list of the things you have dreamed of doing but have never attempted because of a fear of failure or a lack of self-assurance.

- Share each desire with the Lord, asking Him to confirm to you which ones are from Him. Then lay out the steps you need to take in order to accomplish them.

"Take delight in the Lord, and he will give you the desires of your heart" (Psalm 37:4).

▶ Plan for success.

- Anticipate any obstacles to accomplishing your goals and desires and plan strategies for overcoming them.

- Think of yourself achieving each of your goals and doing the things God has put on your heart to do.

"May he give you the desire of your heart and make all your plans succeed" (Psalm 20:4).

▶ Celebrate each accomplishment.

- Your feeling of self-worth and self-confidence will grow with the acknowledgement of each accomplishment.

- Rejoice with the Lord and other significant people over the things God has done through you and for you. Affirm and celebrate your success.

"There, in the presence of the LORD your God, you and your families shall eat and shall rejoice in everything you have put your hand to, because the Lord your God has blessed you" (Deuteronomy 12:7).

▶ Envision a ministry.

- Allow your mistreatment to be the making of your ministry.

"Praise be to the God and Father of our Lord Jesus Christ, the Father of compassion and the God of all comfort, who comforts us in all our troubles,

so that we can comfort those in any trouble with the comfort we ourselves receive from God" (2 Corinthians 1:3–4).

- Don't be consumed with negative messages you may have received from others.

"Forget the former things; do not dwell on the past. See, I am doing a new thing! Now it springs up; do you not perceive it? I am making a way in the wilderness and streams in the wasteland" (Isaiah 43:18–19).

Mistreatment is no stranger to any of us. Why then, in the face of misfortune, do some victims see themselves as having little value, while others live victoriously in light of their true value? What makes the difference?

The victorious Christian learns priceless lessons through mistreatment. Be consumed with the positives you have received from God and can pass on to others.

The blessing comes when you focus not on what you are getting, but on what you are giving. Jesus suffered immense mistreatment, yet He was not burdened with low self-worth. His ministry of compassion models for us the truth that truly ...

"It is more blessed to give
than to receive."
(Acts 20:35)

Everyone has been touched either directly or indirectly by some form of victimization. That means all of us are in a position now or will be in a position in the future to further a survivor's journey on the way to becoming an overcomer, to travel from merely coping to thriving, from struggling to winning, from pain to peace, and from victim to victor.

As you travel that road with someone dear to you, make it your goal to ...

▶ Listen with your heart, without judging, without questioning.

▶ Believe what you hear, without doubting, without qualifying.

▶ Validate the injury, the feelings, the pain, and loss with words, with emotional responses, with actions.

▶ Comfort with compassion, with words, with Scripture, without pity.

▶ Encourage counseling, group support, sharing the secrets.

▶ Learn about victimization, about the healing process.

▶ Strengthen in the Lord, with prayer, with Scripture.

- Express your thoughts, your feelings, your goals, your boundaries.

- Support the healing process with time, with words, with actions.

- Respect the commitment to healing, the time healing takes, the space healing requires, the process of healing.

- Accommodate progressive changes, flashbacks, anger.

> *God heals the broken heart*
> *when you give Him all the pieces.*
> *He washes the wound,*
> *mends the mind, tallies the tears.*
> *He empowers you to rise above abuse*
> *and become all He created you to be.*
>
> —June Hunt

SCRIPTURES TO MEMORIZE

How am I to **bear up under the pain of unjust suffering**? Is there an **example** for me to follow?

*"It is commendable if someone **bears up under the pain of unjust suffering** because they are conscious of God. ... To this you were called, because Christ suffered for you, leaving you an **example**, that you should follow in his steps."* (1 Peter 2:19, 21)

Where was the **Lord** when I was so **brokenhearted** and **crushed**?

*"The **Lord** is close to the **brokenhearted** and saves those who are **crushed** in spirit."* (Psalm 34:18)

How can I look forward to the future and know that God will make my **path straight** when the path of my past was so devastatingly crooked?

*"Trust in the Lord with all your heart and lean not on your own understanding; in all your ways submit to him, and he will make your **paths straight**."* (Proverbs 3:5–6)

Where can I **find** the **rest** and the **hope** that **God** promises to those who trust in Him for **salvation**?

*"Yes, my soul, **find rest** in **God**; my **hope** comes from him. Truly he is my rock and my **salvation**; he is my fortress, I will not be shaken."* (Psalm 62:5–6)

Does the Lord have any **good news** of **freedom** for me, an **oppressed prisoner** of a painful past?

*"The Spirit of the Lord is on me, because he has anointed me to proclaim **good news** to the poor. He has sent me to proclaim **freedom** for the **prisoners** and recovery of sight for the blind, to set the **oppressed** free."* (Luke 4:18)

When someone in my life **sins**, is it okay for me to **go** to them **and point out their fault**?

*"If your brother or sister **sins**, **go and point out their fault**, just between the two of you. If they listen to you, you have won them over."* (Matthew 18:15)

Can God's **Word** actually **heal** my damaged emotions and **rescue** my life from what seems like a **grave** of hopelessness and insecurity?

*"He sent out his **word** and **healed** them; he **rescued** them from the **grave**."* (Psalm 107:20)

How **will** I ever **be free** from the pain and damage of my past?

*"If the Son sets you free, you **will be free** indeed."* (John 8:36)

Am I to **forgive** a **grievance** I have **against someone** who has mistreated me?

*"Bear with each other and **forgive** one another if any of you has a **grievance against someone**. Forgive as the Lord forgave you."* (Colossians 3:13)

NOTES

1. *Merriam-Webster's Collegiate Dictionary*, electronic edition (Merriam-Webster, 2001).

2. James Strong, *Strong's Hebrew Lexicon*, electronic edition (Online Bible Millennium Edition v. 1.13) (Timnathserah Inc., July 6, 2002).

3. Malcolm Smith, *No Longer a Victim* (Tulsa, OK: Pillar, 1992), 9–10.

4. Candace Walters, *Invisible Wounds* (Portland, OR: Multnomah, 1987), 62.

5. Ellen Bass and Laura Davis, *The Courage to Heal: A Guide for Women Survivors of Child Sexual Abuse* (New York: Harper & Row, 1988), 49.

6. Rich Buhler, *Pain and Pretending* (Nashville: Thomas Nelson, 1991), 65.

7. Bass and Davis, *The Courage to Heal*, 213, 217–219; Joyce Meyer, *Beauty for Ashes: Receiving Emotional Healing* (Tulsa, Okla.: Harrison House, 1994), 29–30.

8. Carmen Renee Berry and Mark W. Baker, *Who's to Blame? Escape the Victim Trap & Gain Personal Power in Your Relationships* (Colorado Springs, CO: Piñon, 1996), 35–40, 52–58.

9. Berry and Baker, *Who's to Blame*, 49–60; Lynda D. Elliott and Vicki L. Tanner, *My Father's Child: Help and Healing for the Victims of Emotional, Sexual, and Physical Abuse* (Brentwood, TN : Wolgemuth & Hyatt, 1988), 7–8.

10. Walters, *Invisible Wounds*, 62.

11. Buhler, *Pain and Pretending*, 65.

12. Elliott and Tanner, *My Father's Child*, 9–12.

13. Karen Randau, *Conquering Fear* (Dallas: Rapha, 1991), 44.

14. H. Norman Wright, *Anger* (Waco, TX: Word, 1980), audiocassette.

15. Wright, *Anger*.

16. Lawrence J. Crabb, Jr., *Understanding People: Deep Longings for Relationship*, Ministry Resources Library (Grand Rapids: Zondervan, 1987), 15–16; Robert S. McGee, *The Search for Significance*, 2nd ed. (Houston, TX: Rapha, 1990), 27–30.

17. Gary Jackson Oliver and H. Norman Wright, *When Anger Hits Home* (Chicago: Moody Press, 1992), 97.

18. Wright, *Anger.*

19. Crabb, *Understanding People*, 15–16; McGee, *The Search for Significance*, 27.

20. Wright, *Anger.*

21. Crabb, *Understanding People*, 15–16; McGee, *The Search for Significance*, 27.

22. Dan B. Allender, *The Wounded Heart* (Colorado Springs, CO: NavPress, 1990), 183–97.

23. Elliott and Tanner, *My Father's Child*, 109–124.

24. Allender, *The Wounded Heart*, 197.

25. Meyer, *Beauty for Ashes: Receiving Emotional Healing*, 52–53.

26. Bass and Davis, *The Courage to Heal*, 134–36.

27. Smith, *No Longer a Victim*, 25–27.

28. Allender, *The Wounded Heart*, 227–29.

29. Doris Van Stone and Erwin W. Lutzer, *No Place to Cry: The Hurt and Healing of Sexual Abuse* (Chicago: Moody, 1990), 90–92.

30. Augsburger, *The Freedom of Forgiveness*, 47–50.

31. Lewis B. Smedes, *Forgive and Forget: Healing the Hurts We Don't Deserve* (San Francisco, CA: Harper & Row, 1984), 21–26.

32. Smedes, *Forgive and Forget*, 23.

33. Alexander Pope, *Essay on Criticism*, part 2, line 325.

34. Augsburger, *The Freedom of Forgiveness*, 44–46.